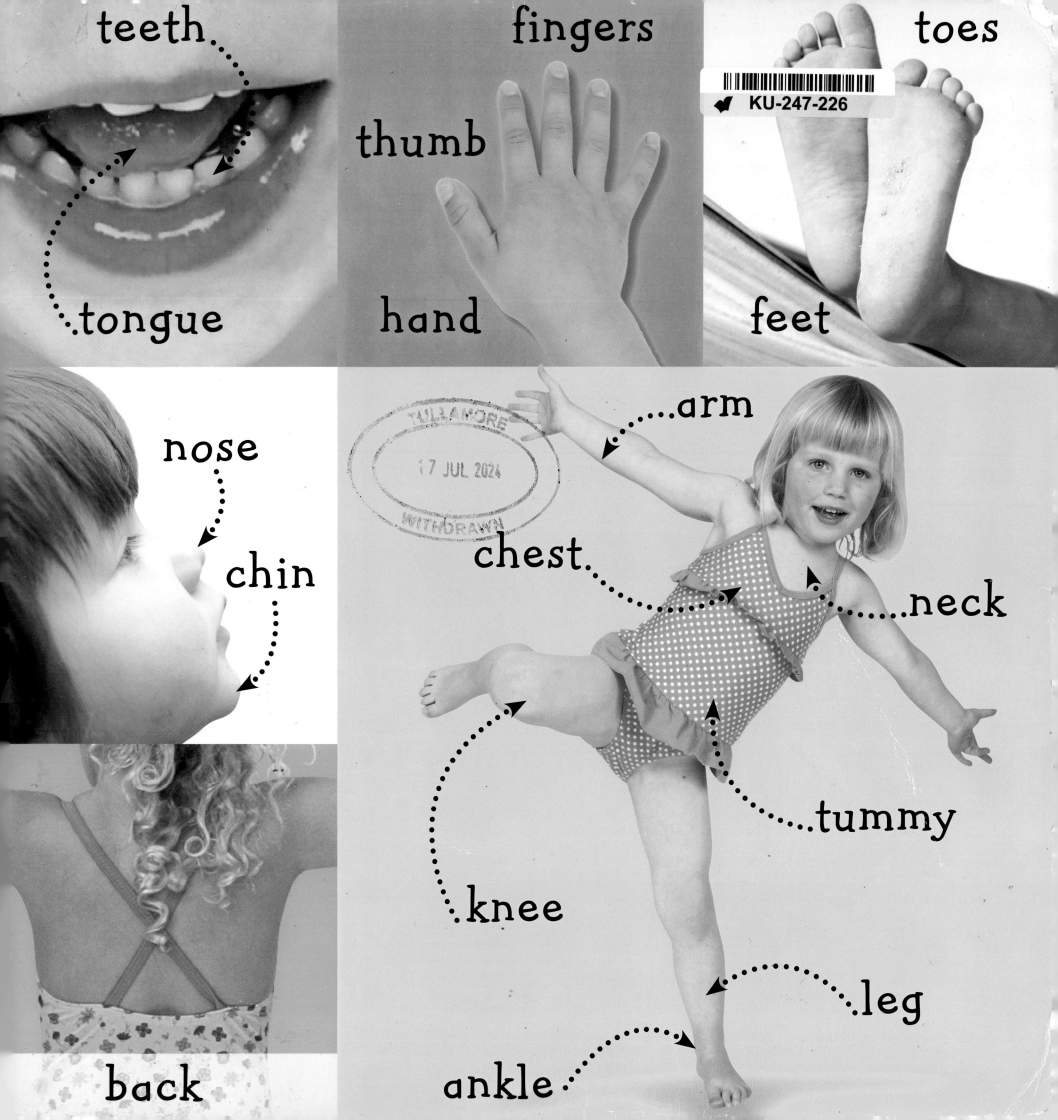

teeth

fingers

toes

thumb

tongue

hand

feet

nose

arm

chin

chest

neck

back

knee

tummy

leg

ankle

Mealtime

peas

cup

carrots

strawberry

cookie

cupcake

cereal

milk

egg

banana

apple

fork

plate

knife

sandwich

Clothes

jumper

shirt

dungarees

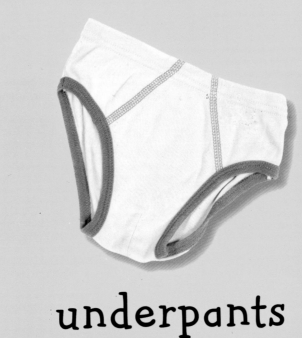

underpants

shorts

shoes

socks

T-shirt